I0134631

CONCENTRIC DEVOTION

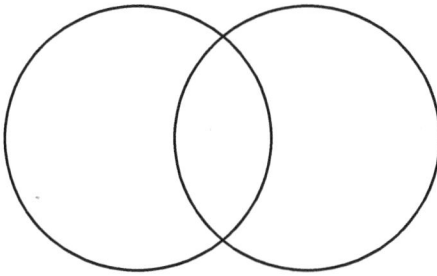

a journey into light

Published by Dreaming Deer Press
Marietta, GA, USA 30067

Copyright © 2014 by Joseph S. Plum
All rights reserved.

ISBN-13: 978-0615971568

ISBN-10: 0615971563

No portion of this book may be reproduced without prior written permission from the publisher, except brief selections for reviews or articles.

Back cover photo of Amelia Plum taken and used with permission by Asa Plum; cover photo of Harlon and Rose Plum taken in 1934, photographer unknown.

Printed in the United States of America

For poetry books, CDs & DVDs
by Joseph S. Plum, please visit:

www.JoePlum.com

Concentric Devotion

the original progression
of vanishing density

Joseph S. Plum

Dreaming Deer Press

Preface

In every era there is a modern age, a revolving world turning beneath our feet. Before nations existed, generations of good people lived in union with nature. When the spoken word reflects this harmony, we are all linked together forming a bond that continues to this very day. Please say these poems aloud. In this way the power and beauty of being human lives on as an event, not simply as a monument.

Artist Statement

"through this pool of living water
the ancestral stream empties into a river
how well the current knows its course
with mountains and oceans both the source"

-Traveler's Rest

There is a power in the spoken word. When any one word is said out loud, say the word "world," that word is being spoken simultaneously all across the globe. This gives a strength and a continuity which sustains us as humans. Add to this a good intent and the word, "world," as any word, can become an active ingredient in creating a healthier place to live. The ancients called this practice harmonious speech.

-Joseph Samuel Plum

Acknowledgments

The poet would like to thank the source of dreams, the givers of song, and all of the upstream swimmers who slipped into becoming that we might begin coming more fully into being. Heartfelt gratitude to the moon and stars, rocks and fire, and to Pat for the vision.

concentric (kən-sĕn'trĭk) adj.

having a shared center

-The American Heritage Dictionary

Contents

for Aerion Cenote

and

for her mother

"today leads into tomorrow

and draws us very near,

rest with ease in wonder

the house of love

has no room for fear"

-from *Landmass Poetry*

cradle

when did the spheres

and the wisdom of spheres

break into parallel lines

then dots and dashes?

too much success

is not an advantage

too much praise

a hostile conspiracy.

soft the grass

beneath the snow

silent winds

from heaven blow

two old souls

suddenly alone

between them

grave mound

no stone.

"to pass away in lightness

on a bridge that leads

is to arrive out of darkness

set to conceive"

-Aerion Cenote

moonlit children

greetings from the starlight tribes
clans of midnight
i am an American Bard
a native bardic poet
speaking for the land
my function is manifold
yet somewhat singular
today, like many days
because we choose it
we are taking part
in a dangerous revolution
for bardic poetry is as revolutionary
as it is dangerous
for bardic poetry is like the kiss of a lover
to one who has half-forgotten love
at once unexpected, always terrifying
yet somehow sweet and entrancing
full of beauty and wonder when first it comes
it comes!
but then it goes
oh, how it goes!

and darkness follows

a leaping sadness in the heart

a questing unfulfilled

a long, strange, aching stillness

which wraps us inside

if you are honest

prepare

prepare now

to ask yourself

"what is this fine breath of air?"

   between the place of living

and the place of dying

i have been walking

past the point of stemming

i have traveled

inbound on the northern tides

through the portal of the regal eyes

wrapped in memory's disguise

within the touch of the white one

my sun soul has arrived

   in the dream silence

the embers keep glowing

though the flame is extinguished

smoke is still rising

while in the high heavens

the star sisters are watching

for the moonlit children to come dancing

through great clouds that are climbing

into a sky laced with soft fingers

eagerly stretching towards the pale light

of a gentler good morning

   and the moonlit children

are talented in ways

not given to nations

or secured in days

and they can feel

a partition in the mind

a blockage of jumbled thoughts

of kin and kind

through which sweeps

a cool, life giving air

a sweeter breeze

for a once darker fare

(hand holds on that sovereign chair).

   who lingers?

half-sleeping in soft repose

or passing among temples of a distant time

or seeking unseen some future sign

what is this fine breath of air?

this ageless gift from we know not where

this sightless path scented

with honey vapor of silken tongue.

if it pleases the gods

may it be a truth

that love and destiny

are one.

embryo nation

now

i don't know who here

will agree with me

sometimes though it seems

as if the greatest part of each of us

actually exists elsewhere

and what you know of me

and what i see of you

is simply the smallest portion

of a much larger, greater whole

therefore when we gather together

(as we have here today)

through our thoughts

and through our feelings

we bring into being

into these realms

those who actually exist elsewhere.

yes, today is for the ones

who wait between the gates

where the inner city secret

meets the world of fates

where the unformed energies

of the embryo race

first begin to accumulate

into a sense of being

that memory can illuminate

once pure light begins to illustrate

the qualities which make life great

for we are all born children of the air

then brought to earth by uncertain despair

where we must now spin and weave

and contemplate

endeavor to outmaneuver

our earthly fate

   where is the village

of the dwellers within ?

home to the weavers of the weft

and the transformer of men

where are the steps leading

into the temple at the hollows of the wind?

where the white star warrior waits

for time to begin again

as an ocean of tides laps against the sky

at this world lands end

and the lords, and the ladies

from the realm of no dominion

drift off into sleep listening

for the footfalls of their long gone

yet never quite forgotten friends

    where is this village of the dwellers within?

if you seek to belong to a time half-remembered

in answer to the urgings of your future kin

then enter now through the sound and the service

of the circle eternal

to be drawn into the open center

of the universal internal

and therein stand

to be made welcome

by the birthless assemblage

from the starlight tribes

midnight clan!

greetings

from the starlight tribes

clans of midnight

i am the assembler

of the prospect of the notion

the enchanter

of worlds yet unspoken

the weaver

of a web whose thread

passes through me unbroken

the articulated embodiment

of unexpressed emotion

the leveler who comes here

with heart and hands wide open

for yes, i am the assembler

the fifth portion

who has gathered the seeds

that have been eons in the sowing

who has captured the thoughts

which keep the knower from the knowing

who has harvested the silence

from which these words keep on flowing

that through hearing

understanding may lead

into a feeling which is forever showing

infallible instinct to be the source

of all things alive and growing

    greetings

from the starlight tribes

clans of midnight.

    on this earth

our feet are resting

in the distance

our eyes have settled

across the horizon

our thoughts are now reclining

    oh, how the crickets

and little frogs were singing

in those first days

of an early autumn

winter's silence

came soon upon them

they could feel

the cold night returning

beneath the leaves

they stayed on their journeys

while here on this earth

their feet were resting

    who will listen

for you at sunset

and carry your shadow

towards the dawn

no one knows

the steps you have taken

or the way in which

i am going

to greet the sun

when beneath the clouds

on a mountain of dreams

our feet are resting

as the twilight reign begins

while in the fields below

the homeless are whispering

to each other in the wind

they say that the green

is all too quickly leaving

that their time in this world

has reached an end

then turning to me

with gentle faces

they ask

will you not come with us

into the heartland

of all places

and watch

as our children drop

from beneath our skin

do you not know

the voice of remembering

that leads across

a threshold

into the home

of the wolf

who is a friend

you do not know

that here on this earth

our feet are resting

while far away

into the future

our spirits have been

to teach ourselves

the songs

the little ones are singing

that we might call them

back from the silence again

when on the edge of extinction

we travel together

to clear out the pathways

for the passing

of a few true men.

    all but forgotten

this forever dwelling

this horseless rider

whose heart is galloping

towards the ragged throats

of winter

never begotten

by skillful arguing

this childlike offering

which insists on telling

of prenatal ancient beginnings

underlying

every physical sensation

undying

in the face of seasonal change

time out of mind

we will again become blessed

as we become "us"

once ignited by design

the light in the eyes

of the unnamed one

flames up.

    born of the blood

of burning desire

on the tip of my tongue

is the taste of fire

as these words each turn

to ashes then dust

birth follows death

as always it must

spoken in the hopes

of renewing a vow

while drawing shade

out of shadow

a language of light

was released somehow

it was a question of harmony

focused on a movement within

and although

the answer was balance

the solution

is brought about

by listening

to the gospels of the wind.

    alone

each of us has been left to find

a thread that unravels

the fabric of space and time

not to be afraid

is very hard to do

when heaven and earth

in all their might

have made only one of you

as the momentum of generations

begins to unwind

the spirit who moves

steps forward to redefine

the principle commitment

that connects body to mind

and then shadows

from the moon and the sun

shall overlap

while the multitudes from creation

speak up

on their own behalf

so that after the touch

of those who are

much more than us

all that remains

to be expressed

is that in the old gods

the young ones must trust.

     no dream nor fantasy

not unspoken desire

can bring to the forefront

the virtues of fire

like sleeping in the cold

in concert

with being hungry and tired

no fable nor metaphor

or mythological past

can sanctify ritual into a feeling

that the heart can grasp

unless first rooted in heavens

and then in blood held fast

for truth entertains no notion

that will not last.

Aerion Cenote

stay with me
earth's gravity said
to the moon
as the sun was passing by
i'll never leave
promised night time's shadow
to the morning
as a bright new dawn
filled the sky
come back
called out an empty river
to the ocean
leaving on low tide
this is it
cried the still heart
pointing
to an emptiness inside
it's too late
life alone within itself sighed
it's too late
for future generations to hide

it's too late

for anything but goodbye

   don't talk to me of starlight

with a twinkle in your eye

and i won't see life

as sunshine reflected

each night

when the moon is on the rise

know only

that tomorrow holds for us

all reason that will rhyme

with a season of flesh and blood

cradled in the essence of mankind

where one day we shall all

be born again together

from beneath the belly

of grandmother time

and what we are

will be given over

to a tenderness sublime

with the coming of a god-child

who is both forever yours

and will be always mine.

rapidly approaching lavender

heaven and earth are set aside

far horizons receding

reveal bloodlines of emptiness

that blindness can no longer hide

for deep inside shades of gray

that are gathering

behind eyes that can see

only black and white

wrapped in a blanket of stars

eternity's immortals sleep tonight

dreaming in an unknown language

like lost children

from some long forgotten genocide

who are seeking to reawaken

from within their memory

the vision to become

a being filled

with power and might

who together

with our ancestral offspring

give to all of those

who come within their sight

a blessing

which is fertility in motion

the rebirth

of our inherited right

to claim once more

personal sovereignty

over the outer reaches

of inner light

where the origins

of the fires of inner vision

have had the foresight to solidify

into a spectrum of tribal colors

from which truth may be identified

while on a journey to the surface

to be in allegiance

with the primordial alliance

of commodity, firmness and delight

which join together

in this forceful uprising

of twin currents

one of starlight blood

the other,

the love of life.

   so is it Celtic

or is it Shoshoni

that put the stars

above me

instead of below me

was it the Buddha

or was it the Christ

who opened my eyes

that i might close

them both twice

for i was Egyptian

before it was written

that language would be invented

as a healing prescription

to gather together

light out of dark

to call back from silence

the echo

of a still beating heart

which radiates with power

through the eye of the hawk

who carries on his shoulder

in a shape like a god

a watcher to keep guard

on our innermost thoughts

that our bodies might survive

this earth spirits assaults

as the moment comes quickly

for us to depart

this place of timed beginnings

and endless starts

which lead forever inward

but never down

like earthquake cracks

in an earthquake ground

     for i am

Egyptian

   Celtic

    and Shoshoni

  only the hawk

the sun-eyed god

and eternity know me

for i am

earth's echoing i

with silence

on either side

in exile

from the fruitful regions

of the bountiful sky

   where i am

a shaman

in suspension

for i am

a human reservoir

filling

with the flood waters

of another dimension

where i am

a willow bone framework

supporting

this tent of skin

for i am

a crystallized vortex

of unearthly wind

opening

directly into the source

of this vision

which burns within

where i am

a child

gently cradled

against the land

for i am

dark blood running

touching sand

where i am

a rough hollowed

wooden bowl

for i am

a metal hued

tight lipped soul

where i am

a wind drawn

naked eye

for i am

fixed sightless

on an empty sky,

   with half the world

as enemies

this civilization is filled

with fallen leaves

scattered thickly

across the earth

color is not

their only worth

for far beneath

the surface of what we see

ten thousand echoes gather

so patiently

every last one deserving to be first

each of them waiting

for you only

to give them birth

    for wherever

good luck and bad luck

come mixed together

the house of the lords

of the northern star

will stand forever

chief among

the winds at night

is this rush of air

that comes to court

bearing within it
a gift of prayer
for the newborn
of this world's
last twilight
   in the days
which lie ahead
no one knows
what it is
that should be said
it's only in seeking
this earth spirit's release
that our fragile dreams
will ever come
to rest in peace
after traveling
so recklessly
in the early morning light
there comes a time
of reckoning
just before wrong
turns to right
where between

the in breath

and out breath

of each mortal moment

of this heavenly life

there awaits unmoving

the edge of the blade

of the ceremonial knife

ready and willing

to sacrifice

the known

for the knowing

at any price

    shoulder to shoulder

the phantoms stand

wave upon wave

eroding

the summer shores

of this autumn land

where nation after nation

of winter people

arrive on command

emerging

with nothing more

than the sign of passage

in the palm of their hand

while asking

for their place at the table

that the feasting

might begin

with the taste

and the telling of stories

by the tongue of the wind

as gifts of memory

are given

again and again

in keeping with a doctrine

whose very existence depends

on the interrelated aspects

of a transdimensional clan

whose increase is timed

to coincide

with this world's

eventful end

as the first stages

of the age of stardust

overtake

the last days
of the season of man.
  nested deep inside
the heart of each of us
there is a feeling
we must come to trust
for if we are to spread
our wings and fly
first we must give up
all concept
of what it is to die
like caterpillars growing
from within a cocoon
we must face each day
working
to be awakened soon
for not much longer
can these feet survive
this earth bound pace
to which they're tied
before they feel
the need to climb
to transform

then to ride

beneath silken wings

that glide

on effervescent currents

and visionary tides

which give good cause

for the children of the froth

to rise

and greet again

with open eyes

the graceful return

of the titans of the skies.

   now some doubt it

so i've heard

but with no outward

sign to give

we must give our word

and hope that the sound of promise

travels with our voice

far enough to touch those

who like us

have no choice

but to follow

their own thoughts

back

to where it is

that we come from

to reach inside

and grab hold

of the inner one

who might otherwise

never overcome

this tangle of roots

which lie at the base

of the tongue

so as to speak

in a language

shared by everyone

in words composed

of syllables built

with fire and blood

each a flaming symbol

taken straight

from the heartland

of our native sun

where every life

is a glowing ember

waiting for the wind

and the word

to begin to become

a child ablaze

and burning again

in a world

which is forever fueled

with the rhythms

and incantations found

dwelling deep

within the boundaries

of this kingdom

of sight and sound

   for sound is to hearing

as hearing is to words

as words are to dreaming

as dreaming is to living

as living is to dying

each in a different light

gives another meaning

like stairs ascending

from a mute darkness

beyond all remembering

each step in the undertaking

becomes just one more small awakening.

   for from the top

the bottom is hidden

in minute misunderstandings

while from the bottom

the top is given an air

of being too demanding

all the while

the middle awaits

keeping each side

in constant embrace

by giving

the gift of centering

and so it is

that the journey begins

with one foot raised to fall

and brings about

a traveler's sense

of middle

beginnings

end and all

come, dream with me at twilight

of beauty, heart, and home

let our spirits mix together

so that we will never be alone

as we travel along

the cracks of this world

where enchantments

come twice daily

in the hope

of sharing with us

this life

we've come to know

by giving a love

which flows quite freely.

splendid in its isolation

tremendous in its desolation

unequalled in the enormity

of the entire situation

is the overshadowing revelation

that there is no one here at all

who can answer

without the slightest hesitation

their own primal mother's call.

five times lately now

i've been born a man

seven times seven

before that

my breath has mixed

with the air of this land

three times each time

i've arrived at being

who i am

a fledgling fosterling

out to test the wind

if only to prove once again

that futility is the greatest sin.

    with fire

falling back into darkness

on either side of me

blackness

would quickly overtake

all of what i see

if it were not

for these flaming tongues of fire

to light the path at my feet

while in a chant of dreams

hymns of eternity

rise up from restless sleep

hidden in the function

of articulated flowing speech

lies the formless faceless secrets

the greatest of which i keep

closest to the surface

though in all appearances

very deep

and if i were to say it

in just one word

that word

would have to be

now simply be.

    if my memory

serves me well

there is little

left to tell`

more words

always count for less

when the message

is the silence

which follows all the rest

across a threshold of paradox

to become wedged

in the edge

of a vortex of silhouettes

that swirl unceasingly

about an open center

of nothing in particular

unless already hypnotized

into being personalized

as emptiness

and then reduced

again in size

as to be held captive

by the corners of our eyes

until that moment comes

when there can be no compromise

and all that we are

is easily recognized

among the sound and the vision

with which all our kinsman

have been blessed

as the source and the direction

of the universe itself

begins again to coalesce

into this cry of eons

which has gathered in our chest

and so i stand here still

with folded wings

across my breast

to protect my heart

until i can leave this nest

even though i know

i will be risking

at the very best

a long

and uncertain fall

which ends in a time

where i will still exist

tumbling head long

ever deeper

into an endless abyss

unless i can answer

unlike all the rest

my own hawk mama's call.

   when from within

a distant sound

like a storm of thunder
my absent parents'
voice is heard
recreating in an instant
that eternal urge
to join with them
in the elements
of their upper worlds
where this feeling of falling
naturally occurs
as the essence of being
moves outward
once more to merge
on singing wings
which turn the wind
to words
to lift up my body
with unknown verbs
that surge to speak
with action
during times of birth
of people and places
and each one's

own true worth.

    for yes there are feelings

that thoughts

just will not express

until after the myth

of their origins

has been laid to rest

beneath a marker

which contains this epitaph

that here none shall enter

and none shall pass

unless they can answer

each question

before it is asked

and thereby

climb a ladder

of riddle and rhyme

where every next rung

comes twice as fast

for the first one before it

is also always the last

and the language

of absolute nothingness

that the journey

is spoken in

tells all the futures

of every past

in just such a way

that the moment between

will last and last

while creating in the balance

a silence

which separates

the echo of this

from the echoing that

and gives to our feet

a feel for the path

which leads us to where

we've always been at

asleep and dreaming

long after the fact

that we've already awakened

sometime back.

    through many lives

i have been the same

though in each one known

by a different name
like broken links
of an unforged chain
i lie scattered and fallen
like autumn leaves
orphaned by a winter's rain
i wait only for this earth
my body to reclaim
and then the stars in heaven
shall my final extinction proclaim
as is the custom
with the ancients
by saying once
and once only
my original primal name
that i might come
at last to lie
at rest and in peace
beneath the banner
of the all seeing eye
which continues to forever fly
throughout the fruitful regions
of the bountiful sky.

cloud mountain

and so it is

that the mountain

comes to the cloud

and cloud to the mountain

for mountain is ancestor to the cloud

and cloud

child of the parents' breath

and breath

force and will of spirit

and spirit

fire and vapor of life

to fill the oceans

empty your mind

to cleanse the heart

calibrate time

to instruct the eye

open the soul

to cradle

this one single moment

of homecoming

just let go!

very here of forever

child of mine
be the seed
that always flowers
bear the fruits of time
be this moment becoming hours
ripen on the vine
be the sweet that never sours
throttle back your mind
be the voice of ancient powers
carry on this rhyme
be the children
who are the children
born of the promise
that was given
in the gardens of mankind
you are a ballet of shadows
a dance of lights
an earthly landscape
of endless insights
you are a sense of being
living in this time of becoming

you are a deep well of feeling

feeding an oasis of homecoming.

   an offhand notion

awaits to disclose

an umbilical chord of emotion

that when traveled flows

outward through a heart of devotion

to become a tear in the eyes of those

who have just crossed over

from that mother ocean

into this fragile land

where each new vista shows

another kingdom full of fairy tales

ripe with a wealth of stories to be told

in just such a way

that the child within us knows

what lesson it is

this new fable holds

and why the path of understanding

always takes us down that road alone

so as to lead us

through a wilderness of civilization

to where one day - someday

every child of time must go

to stand there on the banks

of a mighty river of realization

in whose waters

the current continues to expose

a seedbed of language

spawned in the sediments of old

an archaic inclination

overtaken during germination

by the context of the whole

reappearing only after incubation

as a deepening appreciation

of the emerging articulation

of unexpressed feeling

where in we as we know us

first began to unfold

rolling like a thunder that is echoing

down the sunlit slopes of a valley

worth remembering

where we are all children

alive and growing

in the homeland of our souls

where throughout the ages

that are assembling

from the source of all beginnings

a newborn sense is stirring

to a voice

which dresses in the dawning

and begins again to journey

in a light that speaks of morning

towards a future

which holds the coming present

until the present comes

wrapped in a sunrise that is a remnant

of a time when we were one

with a season that has been immortalized

in the singing of ten thousand lullabies

which have just now reached us here

in one final push to make it clear

that our last awakening is very near

    in this land of sleeping butterflies

child like infant caterpillars cry

with the hope that we'll be there

listening in answer to their prayer

that's asking us to hear

revelations encased in our inner ear

visions that come clothed

in silken words which appear

spinning cocoons

around every drop of air

while whispering

this is where

the very here of forever

becomes apparent

by giving birth to the here and now

in fulfillment of our ancestors

most sacred vow

that delivers in the offspring of tomorrow

this message of old

as an inborn tongue of silver

calls out to a heart of gold

"child of mine

bring forth into this world

that is ours

a quality divine

by giving to the future

that is yours

the spirit parents of mankind

who are of one voice

that is calling

now

now is the time

to be a child

to do the telling

to be a child of time."

chant down

look
  light now is coming
darkness is ending
  the soul fire is drumming
shadows are dancing
  treetops are chanting
with strange tongues clicking
  far away tomorrow
a message is sending
  look to the sky
a dream now is bending
  stepping from the stars
spirits are descending
  in our hearts
a pathway is open
  with quick thoughts
welcome is spoken
  gone with the rhythm
of a crossing just chosen
  together a home visit
to forever dwelling

here is the moment
of ancient feel touching
there is a taste
of spirit wind blowing
where are the children
bright eyed and excited ?
(playing with the old one
no longer sleeping)
see the spark
in the eyes of the living
noble remnant
all futures weave

a fire is drumming
treetops are chanting
far away tomorrow
with us is dancing

here now memory
another day's promise
there now tomorrow
powerfully pulling

where now the voice
calling us softly?
  in liquid oblivion
 action clear
   first in the air
all around us
   then in the breath
swirling inside
   here now in a whisper
surging to attention
   there now in the silence
of watching tears fall
   look into the darkness
of beyond life knowing
   look
light now is coming!

oracle

just as these words
are like smoke
so the same
my heart is a fire
it's a blood
of forest and wind
that i require
or else as ash
to this earth
i'll soon retire
my crackling flame burnt
of its own desire
without wood and air
i have no choice
no mouth to give
my breath this voice
no sounds to ring
and echo in the mind
bringing forth from silence
many thoughts divine
in the wildness

where wisdom grows

there is a tree

whose fruit

no one knows

on a branch

that separates

day from night

there sleeps there

in solitude

a many splendid delight

among the stones

who have grown

cold and dark

there awaits there

a hidden silver spark

a tongue of light

not yet to be

a birthless blaze

of unmatched poetry.

    down a tunnel

of spirit wings

through a soundfall

of translucent dreams

above and beyond

all earthly things

heaven loves

a wind that sings.

   turn

and greet the sky

where it meets the earth

pour out your feelings

for all their worth

then stay

to touch the hills

as they grow dark

to cry as though

you've lost you heart

blood, hair, flesh, and bone

together

these become as nothing

when the very next wind that blows

comes to claim your breath

for its very own.

falling

in no hurry
i do not wait
for an unthinking thought
to come
by the time
i get to where i am at
there is nothing going on.
so many leaves
feel like falling
with every little breeze
that comes a calling
still they have a job to do
so out on a limb
they stay
until the tree they serve
and the wind
decide they're through.

concentric devotion

there is a story
told by the ancients
a legend of rebirth
and in the telling
there is a saying
that fell from the mouth
of a star
who came to earth
resurrection is never easy
transition hard enough
when gods play like angels
tears and laughter collide
sending out sparks of blood
which flow down
into the open throat
of the waiting volcano
that sleeping, dreaming
restless inferno
the goddess mother
of all creation,

this overwhelming cauldron
of breathless love.
on the slopes
of that sleeping volcano
in a forest land of broken people
old souls prop each other up
standing around
in clumps of dying timber
only their roots feeling tough.
intertwined with the bed rock
where being solid
is not quite enough
spirit vapors
insist upon singing
anthems whose refrains
are not a bluff.
at the center
of every circle
nothing dissolves eternity
into a single moment
of unequalled trust
spinning away
with concentric devotion

any emotion unable

to settle into dust.

    in the skies

above that volcano

alive in the remains

of our ancestral believers

sitting back to back

with the terrestrial weavers

ancient singers

bring threads of song

into relief

for the restless sleepers

who awake with the sound

of lonely freedom

to walk in a world

of hard beauty

where the only direction given

that can be taken

comes through

the birthing of song

and the unfolding of dreams.

water

cleanses this earth

rocks

purify water

fire

releases the stone

myth

returns to memory

memory becomes

mist in the morning light.

About the Author

"So much is unknown about the author that to say anything about him at all is to give a false impression of definition. We no longer have words that would describe what he is; our frame of reference is insufficient.

The best we can do is to say that he comes from a time long ago. He survives from the first world into ours, the second, and is made a stranger in his own land. He bears the memory of what once was and invites us to go back with him to the place we once left."

-Jdia

About the Author

Joseph Samuel Plum is a direct descendant of Welsh bards and Native American spirit. He lives in South Central Iowa within a group of trees where he composes and presents oral bardic poetry of original nature. He has been doing this for fifty years. This is his second book.

Books by Joseph S. Plum

RELICS

CONCENTRIC DEVOTION

LANDMASS AND OTHER POEMS

BOOK OF SHADOWS

HUMAN LANDSCAPE

OLD PATH

NOBLE REMNANTS

GATHERING POEMS

www.JoePlum.com

www.ingramcontent.com/pod-product-compliance
Lightning Source LLC
LaVergne TN
LVHW021544080426
835509LV00019B/2829